# SHE. HER. I.

## POEMS

# Tellie Simpson

## AGIAMW, LLC

Cover design and illustrations by Annia Designs

Paperback ISBN: 979-8-9856268-2-7
Ebook ISBN: 979-8-9856268-3-4

Library of Congress Control Number:
2022923450

First Edition February 2023

Published by AGIAMW, LLC
www.agirlinamuseumworld.com
Baltimore, Maryland

*Dedicated to all of the beautiful and complex layers of you.*

# To The Readers

When I decided to publish this collection, I was scared. I feared judgment and criticism. But I got over it because I felt compelled to write this book. Not just for myself but for the complex layers that we all have.

*SHE. HER. I.* is my way of helping others peel back those layers to examine and unify them into a rooted form. I wrote these poems at different phases of my womanhood – there's love, pain, healing and growth expressed in each poem. To reach our higher selves, we must first know ourselves – the good, the bad, the ugly and even the really confusing parts. We need to understand what makes us cry, what triggers our anger and what helps us think and act the way we do. I hope this book helps you to reflect, discover or rediscover yourself because we all deserve to be grounded in our greatness.

# Contents

## *SHE*

## *HER*

## I

# Acknowledgments

To my family and friends, thank you.
The "*Hey, how does this look?*"
text messages have ended.

# *SHE.*

I am she. She is me.
Between the scenes and schemes
behind the titles and roles
underneath the rumors and perceived truths
there she lies:
me.

The girl whose scene begins and ends
with every stroke of her pen.
With every word she sheds layers of imitation
saving herself from impersonation.
She is breathtaking.
She is awakened.

She is bound by her words, her truth and her agency.
She has arrived into her
complicated greatness.

*– Tellie Simpson*

TELLIE SIMPSON

*The journey of self-discovery
begins with honesty.*

# *Effort*

She desires to be loved.
He asks, "How may I please you?"
She says, "I do not wish to teach you what should be known."
My body, your skin –
a song that should play
*effortlessly.*

*Love should be experienced by all.*

# *Silence is Golden*

She observes in silence.
She declares
to be judged by silence rather than impulse.
She waits her turn to speak
with value
& with truth.

She observes in silence.
There are messages in silence,
hidden,
mysterious,
necessary.

***There is power in silence.***

*The quieter you become,*
*the more you can hear.*

# *Listen to Her*

She does not mean what she says.
She says, "Stop."
But she means deeper.

Deeper to the abyss,
deeper to the root of her problems.
She does not mean what she says.
She says, "This is too much."
But she means she's addicted – to your
aroma of deep cider and ginger
it lingers on the tip of her nose.

She does mean what she says –
stay.

*When you find true love,*
*hold onto it.*

# *False Image*

She lives within herself.
She lives trapped by society's forced image.
She wants to be lusted and desired
not trapped and misconstrued,
bounded by womanly duties.
She lives for the day she will be reckoned with.

The thrill of pain feeds her.
Lust is on her brain.
Torture him is what she feels.
She knows he wants her to wife
but she does not care.
She lusts for lust,
she lusts for pain, torture and authority.
"Give me pain," she says.

**For pain is how she escapes.**

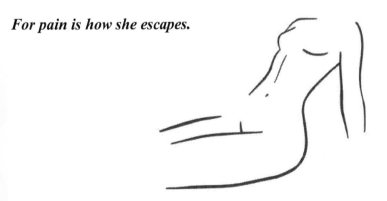

*Serve your body with what it needs and wants.*

SHE. HER. I.

*True freedom is choosing
what's important to you.*

# *Unhinged*

She knew this was what she wanted.
Why was she hesitating?
She dreamed about this
She craved this
But she felt wrong.
*Sometimes the things we want*
*are not always what's right for us.*

She stopped and refused to walk
through the doors.
*Back away and run.*
*Save yourself!*

There she is running.
Running from what?
The answer is not clear
but running away feels right.
Running away feels free.

She runs to escape
Escape the chains
Escape the hold of the mind
Escape the suppression of hiding
who she truly is.

Running away is not a cowardly act.
It is an act of preservation
It is honorable.

She honors herself
by running,
& resisting
to turn the knob to any door that is
unhinged.

*The door meant for you will open.*

*Seductive. Homey. Educated*

# *Deadly Blend*

Hate did not fill her heart whenever
his name was spoken
and she was not angered by the hurt he bestowed
to the heart he said he loved.

Disgust is what filled her mouth
when his name filled the air.
She tasted the sour and tart
reminder of the stabbed wound,
jabbed repeatedly &
healed with the same bandage
he used the first time he inflicted his infection.

The same wound –
never given the chance to heal
stabbed and bleeding
not blood, but agony.
Suffering oozed from the slash.

She screams, "Why do you keep doing this to me?"
"Because you allow it," he whispers as he slowly
pulls the blade from the heart he said he loved.
"Your door revolves, and it never closes."
*You must like it, he says.*

She weeps as she watches him destroy
the love he said he needed.

She weeps,
not for her heart
but for the time lost
on a soul she once knew.
She was once cherished
she was once worshiped.
Lust for affection has left her ignorant,
she now perishes in the
puddle of trauma.

***Love and ignorance do not mix.***

*It's ok to jump ship.*

SHE. HER. I.

*When you undervalue what you do,*
*the world undervalues who you are.*

# *A Daughter's Cry*

Daddy said, "I'll be right back."
15 years went by
until she saw her father again.

She grew up fatherless, but
unfazed by his absence –
at least, that's what she said to the
thoughts that clouded her mind at night.
"*Stop. You don't need him,*" she would say as she grabbed
her head to stop the rowdy voices she heard.

The New York City streets became
the place she would use to fill the void
and ignore the voices.

The taxi horns
the catcalls
the rats scurrying through the trash
flow through her ears.

The streets never lied to her.
They didn't abandon her.
The rats, taxis and the catcalls
were there every night.

& every night she was there listening for his voice to answer her call:

*"Daddy come home."*

**– A fatherless child**

*The right people
never abandon you.*

# *Moonlight*

The moon sees that she's unhappy.
She knows the moon
better than she knows herself.

The moon is the home
she was taken from as a child.
The memories of her being ripped
from her mother's bosom stalk her dreams.

Taken to a foreign place
forced to be amongst humans with no humanity
only vanity.

In this place, love is a facade
and the amount of material things you own
determine if you are worthy.

She yearns to be home
where you are judged by your center.
She follows the light of moon
wishing to return home.
She lets the rays of the
moon direct the next step.
She knows the moon is wise and filled with stories from the
ancestors.

  *– Trust no one; only the light of the moon.*

*Trust your instincts.*

# *The Battlefield*

There she sits
waiting to be rescued
secured and bound to safety.
Mama said that every little girl deserves
a knight in shining armor.
To bring her roses, yes.
But more so to retrieve the woman buried inside.

She's there,
hidden,
ready for the one
worthy of the battle.

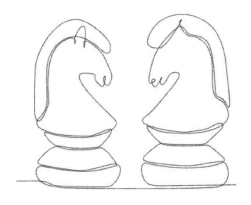

# *Worthy*

The facade is easy to see through
the feelings she carries are made of glass
and she wears them on her sleeve.
It's clear to see that
she is not ok.

She pretends
and mends her feelings so that no one will see
the torment she buries
for her unborn child
for the unprotected Black woman.

*"Everything is fine."*
She repeats this line from morning to dusk.

She must be ok because she said so.
The world knows that this Black woman is not ok.
Yet, they choose to ignore.
"She is resilient," they say.
"She has skin tough as an ox," they cheer.

She is not ok.
She too is worthy of
softness
compassion
& care.

SHE. HER. I.

Take time to care for the Black woman.
***She is worthy.***

*Believe in yourself
when no one else will.*

# *Forward*

As she steps into her soft era
she sheds the past
& releases the regret
it's only making her grow bitter.
Closing the door to her heart is no longer an
option. Love,
security
forgiveness
& abundance are solely welcomed.

**It is time.**

*The past is a place to learn from,*
*not live in.*

# *Core*

"Who are you truly?"
"What do you expect from the world?"

She ask these questions while looking
at the white walls in her bedroom
but she can never answer them.
She is clouded by the body and face
she wears for high society.

Her ancestors write on the wall,
"Strip that face, my child."
"Why do fight the truth?"
"Your core is where you will find the answers you seek."

She repeats, "*My core is where I will find the answers I seek.*"
She slits her wrist;
the red puddle flows as she waits
to find her center.

The core is where life will begin.
**She will be reborn.**

*A fresh start begins with a new mindset.*

# *For the Streets*

The love they shared was a forgery.
He didn't belong to her.
She begged him to stay,
She needed him to stay.
He told her beautiful lies that
she only wanted to hear from his lips.

They felt good,
They tasted good.
*Why are things that are so bad for you taste so good?*

His body kept the bed warm at night.
His heartbeat filled her veins with life.
She needed him more than he needed her.

She felt higher whenever they joined as one.
With him is when she felt closest to her dreams.

They loved they shared was a fabrication.
He shared this love with her and her, and her too.
He was for the streets
& there is where she will leave him.

She will not yield.

*Fake love is just words
and nothing more.*

*Healed. Evolved. Rooted*

# *Her.*

She's not looking for a man to save her
and bring her roses.
She wants the woman momma told her she would be.
Fearless,
strong,
brave,
doing whatever is pleasurable for the day,
for the moment.

She will set the world on fire
with that woman.
She must find *HER*.

*Sometimes the answers we need are in the questions we ask.*

# *Familiar*

I shed a tear.
It sheds for her.
For her buried pain that she does not share.
For her dark thoughts she keeps locked away.

I've heard stories about her,
deceptive, forged & fabricated.
*Who is this woman they speak of?*

*Why does she feel familiar?*

I shed a tear
because: I am HER.

SHE. HER. I.

*Stop running from yourself.*
*Face it all.*

# *Sunup till Sundown*

Her side of the track doesn't shine like gold. Take a walk on her side and you'll see. You'll see her laying the soil to plant her fruits. You'll witness sweat dripping from her face as she works from sunup till sundown. Her side of the track doesn't shine like gold. Take a walk on her side and you'll see. You'll see her carrying a bushel of corn to feed her young & pulling a wagon filled with healed trauma. She pulls the wagon every day as her reminder of how far she has come.

Her side of the track doesn't shine like gold.
Take a walk on her side and you'll see.

SHE. HER. I.

*Your path will lead you to a unique destination.*
*Keep steady.*

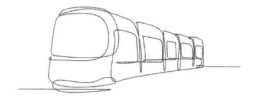

# *Staying In*

No.
A word that rushes from her mouth, eagerly.
Sometimes a little too quickly?
*Nah!*

The word "No" is her superpower.
It protects her from her impulsive decisions.
Her "No" is emotionless to you
but thoughtful for her.

Say it loud for the people in the back,
"No" means:
Her boundaries are sacred.
Her time is precious.
Her hobbies are a necessity.
Her mentality is suffering.
Her body craves affection.
Her spirit needs healing.
Her ancestors are calling.
Her eyes need rest.
Her heart is aching.
Her skin needs moisturizing.
Her gut needs laughter.
Her hands need to create.
Her ears need silence.

Do you want to hang out tonight?
– *No.*

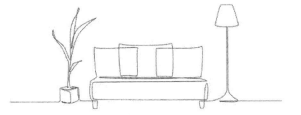

*Home should be a sanctuary.*

# *Guide Her*

Give her unconditional love.
Do not expect her to not make mistakes.
Her love is pure
& fragile.
Her protection may be overbearing at times.
But she fears losing what she cherishes the most –
her sanity.
Sometimes she strays from her destined path
because she loses hope.
Be patient with her and gently guide her back home.

*To find yourself,*
*think for yourself.*

# *Rhythm*

The music rings in her ear
drowning out the emotions.
With every beat of the drum
her heart pounds faster
trying to catch the rhythm and flow.
Her fingers tap with the melody.
Her exhale releases the pain from yesterday,
& heart finds its pace.

*– Find the rhythm of your heart.*

*Music is medicine for the soul.
When you can't find the words,
play a song.*

# *Masterpiece*

Her body aches for his touch.
She wishes for their hands to be joined together
and for their bodies to be entwined between the sheets
creating a masterpiece.

Master and Peace.

Her mind desires to be tamed by him.
For he is her peace.
Her mind,
her body,
will not rest until that space with him becomes her reality.

TELLIE SIMPSON

*Master peace.*

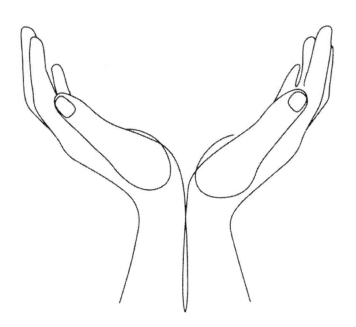

# *She. Her. I.*

She rises from her cursed bed,
with thoughts of violence in her head.
A flash of rage and she sees red.
Without a pause I turned and fled.

I look back to see her grab her head
So I turn back to help her instead.
Her mind is tormented with nightmares
& she never sleeps.
She screams, "Revenge is a promise a girl should
keep."

I know I should run and hide from people like her –
who are filled with anger and rage.
But deep down
I know that we are all trapped
by someone's cage.

Her pain is my burden
& I will not abandon my mission.
Her pain is my ammunition.

*Pull the trigger on anything
that doesn't serve you justice.*

# *Wait for Me*

Her granddaddy told her to go school
and be all that she could be,
to chase the American dream and get educated.

He told her to stay away from boys with fancy cars and lots
of money because they only wanted her sweet fruits.

Granddaddy told her to listen to her teachers and follow the
rules because rules create great players.

He told her to keep a garden
and to grow her own plants
because gardens nurture their owners.

He told her to remember all of his lessons
& to write them down
because one day he wouldn't be around.

He told her this day would come
but to not be sad.
He'll be waiting for her in the garden.

*Every flower must
grow through dirt.*

# *Ordinary People*

I have to let her go.
That's the only way she'll learn
to be independent.
For too long she has kept herself hidden.
Her beauty is only seen by the mirror
that hangs in her bedroom.
Her words only heard by the birds
that wait by her window.

I've sheltered for many moons –
for her protection
because the world can be a cruel place
& if you are not strong enough
it will eat you alive.

The world needs her strength
She needs to know that she matters
and that her presence is needed.
Her courage is like no other:
The way she fights her demons in face-to-face combat
is heroic and angelic.
The world needs to meet her
so they can see that
heroes are just ordinary people who choose to overcome.

*Stop dimming your light
and go blind the world.*

# *Inner Child*

No one ever told her
that her innocence would be snatched away,
stripped from her like cattle from their young.

No one ever told her that her self-worth would be
questioned and ridiculed by her thoughts.
Her worst enemy is herself.

They throw stones at her and she lets them.
Her judgment has declared damnation on her life.

*When did this harsh treatment of herself begin?*
*Why does her worth degrade more and more as each day*
*passes?*

Only one can answer those questions.
*– Her inner child.*

That child is innocent and has no regard
for opinions, judgments or the naysayers.
Her inner child will save her from her destruction.

*Heal your lost inner child.*
*She has suffered enough.*
*Let her rest and guide you to peace.*

# *Infectious*

# *Be Afraid*

I fear judgment. I fear ridicule, failure and abandonment. I fear that I have lost my way, and I've neglected myself for the sake others – others who want to be in my shoes, but do not understand the weight I must carry for the standards I must maintain. Fear can be a bitch, but it can also be a teacher. Fear gives you the courage to face what holds you back. I welcome the fear because, with it, I am the strongest I've ever been.

SHE. HER. I.

*Be scared
and do it anyway.*

# *Arrival*

I have arrived.
I fumbled, stumbled, and I did bend.
I bent my mind for them.
I bent my soul for him.
I fumbled, stumbled, and I did bend.
But I have arrived,
with domination and authority as my shield.
I may stumble, I may fumble,
but I will bend no more.

*Stand strong in your
complicated greatness.*

# *Reflection*

The mirror is shattered on the floor.
Pieces of my reflection lie scattered.
I see myself.
I am flawed
& molded by hands other than my own.
I let them
control me, use me,
shape me into something I didn't recognize.

But I cannot blame them.
A dog will be a dog,
A duck, a duck,
A devil, the villain.
I must take CONTROL.

*– Pick up the pieces and bond them back together with domination.*

SHE. HER. I.

*Mirrors never lie.*

# *Bedtime Stories*

I have many stories to tell.
I tell them all
without fear,
without judgment.
I have stories to share,
stories to lend,
stories to be told over and over –
till I'm ready to begin anew.

I have stories to tell.
I listen to them without fear.
I listen to them without judgement.
I hear them without complaining.

My stories are the reason why –
I'm dying.

*– The lies I tell myself to sleep at night.*

*Pretending to live doesn't make you alive.*

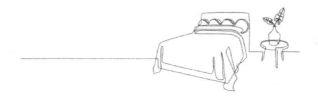

# *Curved Lines*

I do not fit in a box.

I am not a square with sharp edges and lines of precision.

I am curved like waves

floating freely and vivaciously.

I do not fit in a box.

I am not four walls.

I have layers,

no straight boarders or dashes.

I have curved lines that are never-ending.

I am a new form.

*She is rooted but she flows.*

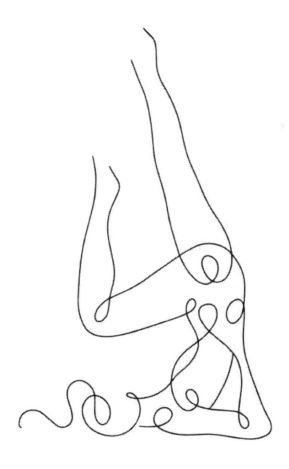

# *Last Supper*

Our love has changed.
I no longer crave his hands on my body.
His words have no effect.
The language he speaks no longer heals.
His speech sounds like a wolf in heat
and I'm ready for the hunt,
to kill him as he did the love I showered him with.
He will never feast on an innocent heart again.

*– I was his last supper.*

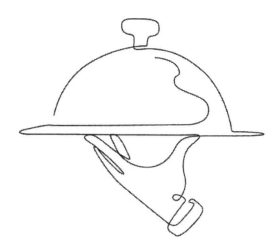

*Guard your heart.*
*Everyone does not deserve access.*

# *Toxic*

I do not stay because I love him
I stay for comfort
for convenience.

He does not truly love me
& his love isn't like the love
my momma told me about.

His love is a disease,
one that grounds itself in
your insecurities and trauma.

I do not need his love.
But his attention is all that is present in this moment  &
in this moment I desire to be desired –
even if it's poison.

*A poisonous love can be a deadly addiction.*
Put the vial down.

SHE. HER. I.

*Find the courage to step
outside of your comfort zone.*

# *End of the Rainbow*

The deep sorrow consumes me.
I drown in the memories
& reminisce on the times we shared floating on the clouds
making snow angels from
the love we wore on our sleeves.
Our love oozed from every inch of our bodies.

With every step we took
our footprints remained
leaving a trail of intimacy.

I look back for the footprints
and I try to follow the path
hoping it will lead me back to you.

With every step I take
comes more pain and misery
but I press on,
hoping to meet you at the end.
Instead, I met what I knew all along.

*– There is no pot of gold at the end of the rainbow, only
the truth.*

*Baby steps are still
steps toward progress.*

# *Glory*

Glory shall be sung
at the top of the mountain.
I will praise myself for this journey.
I reached for the highest triumph
and glory shall be sung in the morning.

*Glory, glory, hallelujah,* I sing.
I fell, but
*glory, glory, hallelujah:*

**I survived.**

SHE. HER. I.

*The climb will be tough,*
*but the view will be worth it.*
*Don't give up.*

# *Chaos*

I like it this way
trapped in my mind
with my fantasies & sinister thoughts.

No one judges me there
& no one is welcomed.
It's a cold, dark place.

There are no field of roses
only thorns and weeds
I thrive in this environment
because where there is chaos
there is a need for it to be mastered.

*– FIND THE CHAOS INSIDE. MASTER IT, and
you will control your peace.*

SHE. HER. I.

*Not all storms come to disrupt your life.*
*Some come to clear your path.*

# *Love Letter*

I wrote a love letter to myself when I was seven.
Love knew me then,
love adored me at that age.
I got older and lost connection with love.
I no longer knew what it looked like
or what it felt like.

*How does one love themselves when they do not know
what real love is?*

I revisit the love letter to myself often
searching for the warmth I once had in my heart.
The letter sits on my night stand every night.
I read it before I open my legs to him.

*"This is it,"* I whisper.
I think I've found love again.
My body grows warmer with every stroke.
We make love till morning.
I open my eyes.
But he's not there.

I grab the letter
& a lighter.

It falls to ground, landing on the carpet.
I watch from the edge of my bed as my room
goes up in flames.

I wrote a love letter to myself when I was seven.
That was last time real love visited my heart.

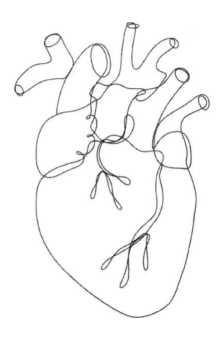

TELLIE SIMPSON

*Love yourself the way you
want others to love you.*

# *Skin*

Being in my own company is my cure.
Sipping my tea under the stars while
wearing my favorite ensemble –
my skin.

There I lie, naked
embellished with joy
& gleaming in my pure form.

I let my bosom hang.
I let my skin soak up the vitamins from the sun
& I watch as the universe cleanses my body
and heals my scars with its tears.

As I take off my clothes
I can see my soul breaking free from the lies I dress up.

The more love I pour into me,
the more my skin will glow.
My naked skin is divine
and I will harm it no more.

*Life is easier when you
are comfortable in your skin.*

# *A Moment*

It's ok to dwell in the pain.
Sometimes you feel like crying
and you don't know why.
That is ok.

I cry tears of sorrow that are
unmotivated by anyone's actions, but my own.
I feel pain caused by my thoughts
& I sometimes I dwell in my misery because I just want to.

But I don't linger there. You cannot linger there.
I pick myself up and find my ray of sunshine.
I tell myself truths that will make me smile again.
I affirm my greatness
and remind myself
that this is not the end.
This moment is simply a moment.

*– You're allowed to have a moment.*

TELLIE SIMPSON

*Everyone has bad days.*

# *Grace*

I give her grace because I didn't
know who she was back then.
I didn't know my skin was tough as nails,
or that my voice was dominating like a lion's roar.
I didn't know that my body could stand so tall
& feel so rooted.

I give myself grace for the
revolving door I had on my heart.
I grew comfortable with the pain
and authentic self-love was nonexistent in my life.

*"Give yourself grace because you know who you are
now."*

I do not stand here embarrassed
or ashamed of my past.
I stand here grounded and proud
in my newfound essence.
I give myself grace
because I am not without flaws.

*Be proud of your growth.*

## *The Villain*

I'll be the villain in your story.
Just make sure you say my name right.

– The victim

*Be the villain;*
*they have more fun and dress better.*

# *My Hood*

Womanhood ain't easy, and it sure as hell ain't boring.
I learned how to walk through fires without getting burned.
I learned skills that helped me pay the bills and put food
in my belly.

I can bat my eyes with such softness and serenity while
my words flow and cut you like a knife – at the same time.
My influence is powerful, but my control is subtle.
You see, those are skills that womanhood taught me.

Womanhood is a true old gangster.
She is a master of all tricks and trades.
If you listen closely, you can learn her ways.

I learned how to get what I wanted by playing this deck of
cards called life and the OG was my teacher.
Womanhood sure ain't easy, but it's the hood I rep.

*To be born female is a divine gift.*

# *Finale*

It's hard keeping up with a face that isn't my own.
When the curtains close and the
audience leaves the building,
there I remain, sitting in the center of the stage
waiting for my next act.
This mask I wear takes a toll on me.
My smile is no longer straight.
It's crooked, cracked and flawed.
The audience grows weary of the same performance.
They think I lack depth.
But underneath my mask lies a delicate soul
who shields herself from the monsters and demons
she read about in her books.
They can look like you and I
but underneath lie their evil intentions.
I am weary of quick smiles and hearty laughs,
so I wear my mask for protection.
Everyone is not deserving of the grand finale.
So I sit in the center of the stage and wait for the curtains to
open to deliver the same performance until
I am ready to reveal my final act –
the woman underneath the mask.

*She transformed into her and created me.*
*I am SHE. HER. I.*

Download the REFLECTION GUIDE for FREE now!

# About the Author

Tellie Simpson has spent her life surrounded by history and art. From visiting and working in museums to being an avid collector, she has carved a space in the Museum field to bring awareness and diversity.

A native of Baltimore, Maryland, Tellie holds an M.A. in Museum Studies and a B.A. in History from Morgan State University. She plans to continue publishing books and spread her love of history, museums, art and culture.

Follow Tellie Simpson on Goodreads for more.

**If you enjoyed this collection, please leave a review.**
Visit agirlinamuseumworld.com

TELLIE SIMPSON

# Other works by Tellie Simpson

*A Girl in a Museum World Children's Book*

*She is Rooted Journal*

*Collect and Preserve Family Treasures*

TELLIE SIMPSON

*If you enjoyed this collection, please leave a review.*

*Download the FREE Reflection Guide to accompany SHE. HER. I.*

agirlinamuseumworld.com

Printed in Great Britain
by Amazon